Momma's Home Cooking

Delicious Southern Recipes & 60 Years of Sage Advice

Wilma J. Miller

To Laura

From

Wilma gmille

10 10 2016

Table of Contents

AUTHOR'S NOTE

I created these recipes from a lifetime of experimentation and hard work. Although I have several vegetarian dishes, I have not honed the same expertise making vegan food—at least, not yet.

Sometime in the future, I will be able to covert traditional Southern recipes into vegan options. Until then, thank you for your patience and your patronage.

Also, we've been very meticulous in testing and editing. If you find an error or have suggestions, we'd love to hear from you!

Email me at: wilma@wilmajeanmiller.com.

INTRODUCTION

I remember my Aunt Greely's kitchen, the first of many kitchens I would use. This was longer ago than I want to admit. Yes, it was a time before microwave ovens were in every home. In fact, it was even before refrigerators were in every home.

I was raised with a gas stove and an icebox that the ice man filled every week.

I rose early to a room so cold that I could see my breath. On most mornings — especially during winter months — frigid wind cut through the uninsulated walls of the kitchen. On the few occasions I was without socks, my young feet felt frozen to the rough wood floor.

I remember water and buttermilk were like ice that numbed my fingers so badly I felt I would never be warm again. At least, I didn't have to pump the water from a well as I had to do when staying with other relatives.

Uncle Robert's house was my home. I had no place else to go.

My movements were slow, sloppy and sleep deprived. I didn't want to be up that early and I certainly didn't want to make biscuits. At twelve-years-old, I had no idea that I would spend most of my life getting up before sunrise to run a machine in a factory or run a kitchen.

After I started water for the coffee, I sifted flour, baking powder, salt, and cream of tartar with stiff fingers. I carefully measured sugar. If I used too much, Aunt Greely would throw a fit. If I used too little Uncle Robert would complain about the taste.

I set the biscuits on the stove for Uncle Robert's breakfast. He was the man of the house and the breadwinner in my adopted family. He would eat the fresh bread before trudging off to work. I had done my part and earned much of my keep for the day.

And make no mistake, I was expected to earn my keep.

Uncle Robert was particular about the food he ate. We all know individuals like him. I've heard of grown men who only ate peanut butter and jelly sandwiches, going as far as to insist on that meal when forced to go to restaurants. Uncle Robert wasn't exactly like that, but he had his quirks.

"You want some banana pudding?" Aunt Greely asked him starting a conversation that was repeated and over.

"Naw," Uncle Robert would answer with a sharp tone. It sounded to me he was offended.

A few moments later, Aunt Greely said, "You want cookie pudding?"

"Why ain't you say dat the first time? Yea, I want some cookie pudding." Under his voice, we could hear him mutter about people wasting his time.

Aunt Greely brought him a bowl of dessert with layers of cookies, pudding — and bananas. It was the same pudding.

At the time, it all seemed very normal to me. I learned not to question Uncle Robert's eating habits. He didn't like canned biscuits. He wasn't going to eat them, so it was my job to cook each morning before school or church.

Making biscuits was my introduction to cooking, something I would eventually come to enjoy doing. From the first moment I stepped into Aunt Greely's kitchen to the moment I put together this book, I've been thinking about ways to save time so I could crawl back into my warm bed.

That thought process carried me through college, marriage, motherhood, and finally, retirement. I've always found ways to stretch my dollar, use less to feed more, and finish quick enough to get on with my day.

Years later, after I started high school, we attended a function at church. Uncle Robert was in a very good mood. He'd eaten his fill and even had some of the biscuits they served. He asked one of the church ladies how she got her biscuits to taste so good.

"They store bought," she said and returned to whatever task she was doing, totally unaware that her innocent comment opened our house to store bought biscuits.

I didn't have to get up early any more.

Cooking is so much more than following recipes or even putting food on the table. Cooking is a way to push yourself to do more with less, to solve problems, and to share in a community of women and men with a common experience.

I put together this book to give you tools you can use to not only make your life easier, but to help you along your own journey.

At the risk of sounding arrogant, my biscuits are pretty good. Try them out for yourself:

Wilma's Southern Biscuits

(makes about 2 dozen)

2 cups sifted flour
4 teaspoons baking powder
1/2 teaspoon cream of tartar
1/2 teaspoon salt
2 tablespoon sugar
1/2 cup shortening, melted
1 egg beaten
2/3 cup of buttermilk

1. Preheat oven to 400°F.

2. Combine sifted flour, baking powder, salt, sugar and cream of tartar in a large bowl and stir well.

3. Make a hole in the center of dry ingredients and add melted shortening, buttermilk and egg.

4. Stir until the dough is stiff.

5. Place on floured surface. Knead about 6 times.

6. Roll or pat to ½-inch thickness.

7. Cut with small round cutter and bake for no longer than 20 minutes or until golden brown.

HOUSEHOLD TIPS

Words of Wisdom

- ✓ Thoughtfulness is always in good taste.
- ✓ Feed your faith and doubt will starve to death.
- ✓ No one knows of your goodness unless you give out some samples.
- ✓ One thing's for sure — if you laugh at your trouble you will always have something to laugh at.
- ✓ Love is the master key that opens the gate to happiness.
- ✓ The Bible is like a bank, it is most helpful when open.

Soup & Stew Tips

- ✓ To absorb grease from the top of a soup, drop a leaf of lettuce into the pot, remove and throw it away; it has served its purpose.
- ✓ If stew is too salty, add round cut white potatoes, discard one at a time. It will absorb the salt. Another remedy is to add a teaspoon of cider vinegar and sugar.
- ✓ If stew is too sweet, add salt to a main dish or vegetable.

Cleaning Tips

- ✓ Baking powder will remove tea coffee stains from china pots or cups.
- ✓ Clean and Deodorize Your Cutting Board Clean it with lemon juice, take away strong odors like onion, or just rub it with baking soda.

Egg Tips

- ✓ If you shake the eggs and you hear a rattle, your egg is stale. A really fresh egg, will sink, and a stale one will float.
- ✓ When making deviled eggs, and wanting to slice it perfectly, dip the knife in water first. The slice will be smooth.
- ✓ The white of the eggs is easiest to beat when it's at room temperature, so leave it out before using it.
- ✓ To make light and fluffy scrambled eggs, add a little water while beating the eggs.
- ✓ To make quick diced eggs take your potato masher and go to work on a diced boiled egg.

- ✓ If you wrap each egg in aluminum foil before boiling it the shell won't crack when it's boiling.
- ✓ To make eggs go further, when making scrambled eggs for a crowd add a pack of baking powder and a teaspoon of water per egg.
- ✓ A great trick for peeling eggs the easy way: when they are finished boiling turn off the heat and just let them sit in the pot with the lid for about ten minutes. Steam will build up under the shell and the shell will just fall away. Or quickly rinse hot hard boiled eggs in cold water, and the shells will be easier to remove.
- ✓ A small funnel is handy for separating egg whites from yolks, open the eggs over the funnel and the white will run through and the yolk will be removed.
- ✓ When baking, it's best to use large to medium eggs. Extra-large eggs may cause cake to fall when cooled.
- ✓ For fluffier omelets, add a pinch of cornstarch before beating.
- ✓ Always heat the frying pan before adding oil or butter to keep eggs from sticking to the pan.

Nut Tips

- ✓ To quickly crack open a large amount of nuts put in a bag and gently hammer until they are cracked open. Then remove nut meat with a pick.
- ✓ If nuts are stale place them in the oven at 250 degrees and leave them there for 5 to 10 minutes, the heat will revive them.

Pasta & Rice Tips

- ✓ Add a lump of butter or a few teaspoons of cooking oil to the water, rice, noodles, or spaghetti will not boil over or stick to the pot.
- ✓ Rice will be fluffier and whiter if you add one teaspoon of lemon juice to each quart of water.

Cheese Tips

- ✓ A quick way to whip cream cheese: add a pinch of salt to the cream cheese before whipping, strengthening the fat cells and making them more elastic so the cream cheese will stiffen much more quickly.
- ✓ Chill cheese before grating and it will take much less time.
- ✓ Tasty cheese sandwiches in a frying pan lightly greased with bacon fat for a delightful new flavor.

Fish & Seafood Tips

- ✓ To keep fish from sticking to the pan, bake on a bed of onions, celery and bell peppers. This will also add flavor.

Bean Tips

✓ When cooking dried beans, add salt after cooking. If salt is added at the start it will slow down the cooking time.

Miscellaneous Tips

✓ Tightly wrap a piece of aluminum foil around the salt shaker. This will keep the dampness out of the salt. To prevent dampness out of the salt keep 5 to 10 rice grains inside
✓ If potato chips lose their freshness, place under the broiler for a few minutes. Care must be taken not to brown them. You can crisp soggy cereal and crackers by putting them on a cookie sheet and heating for a few minutes in the oven.
✓ Boil vinegar in a brand new frying pan to keep things from sticking
✓ Ice cubes will help sharpen garbage disposal blade.
✓ Do not use reduced fat or light margarine when cooking or baking; the results will be disappointing.

LITTLE MONEY &
A WELL-STOCKED KITCHEN

Back in the day we did not have a lot of money, but we ate good all the time.

I studied cooking, I got creative, and sometimes, I prayed. Those three things kept good food on the table.

If you keep the following ingredients you can pull a meal out of your hat. People will think you are a magician.

- Flour
- Sugar
- Corn meal
- Salt
- Pepper
- Rice
- Beans
- Chili powder
- Milk
- Eggs
- Any kind of meat in the freezer

APPETIZERS

A word about appetizers

How can appetizers save you money? You'd think that if you skip the appetizers then you could put those few dollars back in your pocket.

True, but if you think about it, people come to your party hungry. You want to make sure there's plenty of food, but you fill them up on crackers, cheese, and eggs before you bring the shrimp.

Yes, you spend more money, but your money goes further.

Snacking Cracker

You can use hot sauce or any other seasoning you want to.

Make sure to use canola oil only. Any other oil will make the crackers soft.

1 16-ounce package saltine crackers
1/2 cup canola oil
1 package dry ranch dressing
1 tablespoon onion powder
1 tablespoon garlic powder
hot sauce *(optional)*

1. In a bowl, combine crackers and seasoning.

2. Add oil and toss gently.

3. Let crackers set for 2 hours. Overnight works best.

Cheese spread

1 small container pimiento cheese
1 small can (4 - 6 ounces) deviled ham
1/2 cup mayonnaise
1 tablespoon minced onion
few drops Tabasco or other hot sauce *(optional)*

1. Using a spoon, mix pimiento cheese, deviled ham and mayonnaise in a medium bowl.

2. Stir in a onion.

3. You can also add hot sauce to give it a kick.

Deviled Eggs

6 hard-boiled eggs, peeled and cooled
1/2 cup of mayonnaise
2 teaspoons mustard
3 teaspoons pickle relish
1/2 teaspoon salt
1/4 teaspoon pepper
dash cayenne pepper
dash paprika

1. Gently slice the eggs in half length-wise and remove the yolks.

2. In a medium bowl, mash the egg yolks into a fine crumble using a fork.

3. Mix in mayonnaise, mustard, and pickle relish. Add salt, pepper, and cayenne pepper to taste.

4. Chill for at least two hours.

Heavenly Eggs

If you think deviled eggs are good, you gotta try the heavenly version.

12 hard-boiled eggs, peeled and cooled
1 teaspoon Worcestershire sauce
½ cup mayonnaise
1 teaspoon pepper
¼ cup lemon juice
1 pound (16 ounces) mustard
¼ cup sweet pickle radish
1 can (4-6 ounces) diced tomato
1 teaspoon sugar

1. Gently slice the eggs in half length-wise and remove the yolks.

2. In a medium bowl, mash the egg yolks into a fine crumble using a fork.

3. Mix in mayonnaise, pepper, Worcester sauce, lemon juice, mustard, pickle relish, tomatoes, and sugar.

4. Add salt, pepper, and cayenne pepper to taste.

5. Chill for at least two hours.

DIPS

A word about dips

It's easy to dismiss dips. Throw some cheese and chopped tomatoes on a discount bag of chips and call it a day.

I learned that when money is tight you can't experiment with expensive ingredients and spices. If you are new to cooking or you don't have a lot of money, dips are an easy way to get used to cooking.

Take your time. Try new things. Mix it up.

Here's a few tips to remember:

- ✓ Always drain canned meats, beans, and vegetables. Open the can halfway and pour out excess juice before you add to your dip.
- ✓ Do not drain tomatoes. Anything with tomatoes requires the juice from the can the juice from canned tomatoes
- ✓ Always cook meat before adding to a dip. Unless told otherwise, add onions, salt, and pepper.
- ✓ Dice onions in to small chunks. No one likes big onion chunks
- ✓ If your dip is too thick, add milk (whole or 2%, even almond milk works sometimes)
- ✓ If your dip is too thin, you can generally add more cheese.
- ✓ One last thing. Chips and crackers are great, but there are hundreds of different types of breads you can use from all over the world.
- ✓ Never be afraid to try something new and different.

Mex Cheese Dip

Cheese dip was a staple at every party in our house. My husband loved it. My kids fought over it. My friends ate it like it was going out of style. You don't have to use meat. If you do, turkey is healthiest, but beef tastes the best.

1 large (16-ounce) package Velveeta cheese

2 cans (8 or 10 ounces) stewed tomatoes (hot or mild) — I recommend
RO*TEL brand

2 pounds cooked ground meat (turkey, ground beef, or chicken)

1 can (8 ounces) black beans

1 cup of whole or 2% milk

1. Brown the ground meat, adding salt and pepper to taste.

2. Cut cheese into 1-2 inch chunks.

3. In a crockpot or double broiler[1], melt cheese.

4. Stir in cooked meat, milk, and tomatoes.

5. Drain the black beans and stir into the dip.

6. Continue to cook over low heat for 30 minutes, stirring occasionally.

7. Serve hot with tortilla chips.

---

[1] If you don't have a double broiler, use to large pot and a smaller pot. Make sure the smaller pot doesn't have plastic handles.

Deviled Ham Dip

1 can deviled ham
13-ounce package cream cheese
1 teaspoon mustard
horseradish to taste

1. In a medium bowl, mix the ham, cream cheese and mustard. Mix well.

2. If the dip is too thick, you can thin it with mayonnaise.

Chili Dip

2 pounds ground turkey, beef, or chicken
1/2 cup onion, chopped
1 ½ pounds Velveeta cheese
1 tablespoon chili powder
1 can black beans
1 can whole corn

1. Brown and drain the ground meat, adding salt and pepper to taste.

2. Cut cheese into 1-2 inch chunks. Melt cheese in a crockpot or double broiler[2].

3. Stir in cooked meat, chopped onion, chili powder, and corn. Drain the black beans and stir into the dip.

4. Continue to cook over low heat for 30 minutes.

5. Serve hot with tortilla chips.

---

[2] If you don't have a double broiler, use to large pot and a smaller pot. Make sure the smaller pot doesn't have plastic handles.

Spinach Dip

1 package dry vegetable soup mix (I recommend Lipton brand)
8-ounce sour cream
8-ounce plain yogurt
1/2 cup mayonnaise
3 green onions, chopped
1 teaspoon lemon juice
10-ounce package chopped spinach

1. Thaw the chopped spinach and squeeze the packaging to remove excess moisture.

2. In a medium bowl, mix sour cream, yogurt, mayonnaise, onions, lemon juice, spinach, and soup mix.

3. Chill and serve cold.

Taco Dip

1 pound ground beef or turkey
1 package taco seasoning
1/2 cup water
1 pound Velveeta, cubed
1 1/4 cup salsa

1. In a medium sauce pan, brown the ground meat. Add salt and pepper to taste. Drain.

2. Add seasoning and water. Continue cooking until the ingredients are mixed.

3. Slowly stir in cheese and then salsa.

4. Serve hot with tortilla chips.

Shrimp Dip

1 can tomato soup

1 cup mayonnaise

9 ounces cream cheese, softened

1 teaspoon Worcestershire sauce

1/4 cup of green onion, chopped

1/3 cup of celery, chopped

1 1/2 cups (about 3 cans) cooked tiny shrimp

1. In a bowl, mix tomato soup, mayonnaise, cream cheese, and Worcestershire sauce until smooth.

2. Stir in green onion, celery, and shrimp. Chill.

3. Serve cold with chips or fancy crackers.

Chili Cheese Dip

This is a simple dip is so simple, it's almost cheating.

2 cans cheddar cheese soup

2 cans chili with bean

1. Heat together in a sauce pan.

2. Serve with chips.

Shrimp Cheese Dip

Here's another simple recipe.

1 clove of garlic, chopped
1 can cream of shrimp soup
1 can of small shrimp
1 can of mushroom soup
1/2 pound American cheese (cubed) - I use Velveeta

1. In a sauce pan, add garlic, shrimp soup, shrimp, mushroom soup, and cheese.

2. Heat all the ingredients over low heat.

3. Serve hot with chips.

SAUCES

A word about sauces

Saint Louis, Missouri...Chicago, Illinois...Kansas City, Missouri...Austin, Texas...Tallahassee, Mississippi...Little Rock, Arkansas...

Every city and state in the South got its own barbecue. Missouri ribs ain't like Texas ribs, which ain't like ribs in Florida. And none of them like ribs in Arkansas.

What's the difference?

Sometimes it's the cut of the meat, and other times it's the kind of meat. Pork ribs are king, but beef ribs can be amazing.

I've been blessed enough to travel to a few places with friends and family. I've tried barbeque in several states. But there were times I couldn't afford to travel. I didn't have the money or the time.

Even then, I could still make something at home. When we couldn't go somewhere, I brought the place to me. As long as I have that, no place is outside my reach.

I couldn't afford a rack of lamb or a Alaskan crab legs, but I can afford a sauce and when you are starting out, anything is everything.

One day, I might do a book on sauces — until then here are few recipes that are uniquely mine, uniquely Arkansan, and now they're uniquely yours.

Chicken Gravy

Nothing like gravy made from fried chicken. Nothing like it in the world.

If you're not familiar with Southern food, this gravy is perfect over potatoes, chicken, and vegetables.

1/2 onion, sliced

1 cup flour

2 cups water

1. After frying chicken in skillet, remove chicken and pour off oil. Let scraps stay in the skillet and add onion.

2. Slowly stir in flour and let brown. Add water until you get the thickness you desire.

3. Cook for 15 minutes.

4. Remove from heat and let stand for 10 minutes before serving. Enjoy!

Miller Family Special Cue (BBQ) Sauce

½ cup brown sugar
¼ cup paprika
¼ cup chili powder
1 tablespoon onion powder
1 teaspoon garlic powder
1 teaspoon salt
¼ vinegar
1½ cup water
1½ cup catsup
½ cup Worcester sauce
1 teaspoon thyme
1/3 cup lemon juice

1. In a sauce pan, mix all ingredients.

2. Bring to a boil.

3. Lower heat and simmer for 30 minutes.

Me and Jerry
Last Dance Barbecue Sauce

1/2 cup chili sauce

1/3 cup Worcestershire sauce

1 tablespoon onion powder

1 teaspoon garlic powder

1/2 teaspoon salt

1 teaspoon black pepper

¼ cup vinegar

1 teaspoon celery seed

1 tablespoon brown sugar

1 can beer

1. In a pan, place all ingredients except for the beer.

2. Boil over low heat for 30 minutes.

3. Add beer, cook for 10 minutes.

4. Serve as sauce over meat.

Barbecue Sauce

Sometimes, you just need a shortcut....

small (14-ounce) bottle ketchup
small (14-ounce) bottle steak sauce
1/3 cup Worcestershire sauce
1 cup water
½ cup brown sugar
1 tablespoon garlic powder
juice of 1 lemon
1 tablespoon yellow mustard
Tabasco (any vinegar-based hot sauce)

1. In a sauce pan, combine ketchup, steak sauce, Worcester sauce, brown sugar, and water.

2. Simmer over low heat for 5 minutes.

3. Stir in lemon juice, mustard, and Tabasco sauce.

4. Continue simmering for 1 hour, do not boil.

5. Serve with barbecued, smoked, or grilled meat. Goes well with beef, chicken, and pork.

BREAKFAST

A word about breakfast

When we were going over the recipes for this book, I decided to remove most of this section for my Southern Breakfast Handbook. Still, I wanted to put a few recipes in. If you are a beginner in the kitchen, omelets are a great way to gain some cooking skill. If you can flip an, omelet then you can do almost anything else over a stove.

Sweet Potato Hash Browns

3 cups sweet potatoes, diced
1/2 cup onions, chopped
1 cup bell pepper, chopped
1/2 teaspoon salt
1/2 teaspoon black pepper
1/3 cup vegetable oil

1. Heat oil in a skillet on a medium setting.

2. Add potatoes, onions, and peppers. Stir gently while adding seasoning.

3. Cook until done for about 30 minutes.

4. You can cover the skillet to cook the potatoes faster and have less crispy results.

Omelet

4 slices bacon, pork, or ham
1/4 cup onion, chopped
1/4 cup green pepper
4 eggs
1/4 cup whole or low-fat milk
1/2 teaspoon salt
1 cup American or medium cheddar cheese, shredded
4 tablespoons cooking oil

1. In a bowl, whisk eggs and mix in milk.

2. In a 10- to 12-inch skillet, cook bacon or ham. Remove meat, but not the drippings.

3. Sauté onion and peppers in skillet over low heat until tender. Remove vegetables and set aside.

4. Raise heat to medium-low. Pour in beaten eggs. Allow eggs to cook until the bottom layer solidifies.

5. Sprinkle meat, onion, pepper, and cheese on one half of the eggs.

6. When the egg is mostly done, use a spatula to fold the egg in half. Cook for 30 seconds. Flip the omelet a second and heat for another 30 seconds.

7. Remove from heat. Sprinkle cheese on top and serve hot.

Arkansas Style Omelet

Sometimes, eating healthy is the last thing on your mind. I added this recipe for those mornings when you want something to stick to your ribs.

6 slices of bacon

½ cup onion, chopped

½ cup green pepper, chopped

6 eggs

½ cup heavy cream

½ teaspoon salt

1½ cup shredded American or cheddar cheese

1. In 10- or 12-inch skillet, cook bacon

2. Leave drippings in skillet, remove bacon and crumble it in with the mixed onion and green pepper.

3. Place mixture into skillet and cook over low heat until the vegetables are tender.

4. Remove vegetable and bacon mixture and set it aside.

5. Beat eggs, milk, salt and pepper together.

6. Pour egg mixture into hot skillet, add vegetable mixture, then cheese.

7. Let it cook over low heat until it is done. Loosen omelet and remove.

8. Place on large plate, cut and serve.

BEVERAGES

A word about drinks

As you read through this book you will notice a trend. (My son calls it a theme cause he's gotta be all fancy.)

But seriously, if you didn't notice it, I'm going to spell it out in plain language:

Just cause you ain't got much, don't mean you ain't got nothing. I've been to parties where people serving shrimp like it's a dollar a pound. Well, that's not my party.

Since "not much" don't mean "nothing," I can still serve drinks to my friends. I can still have a little get together for my child's birthday.

Always do the best with what you got. People will come over and have fun. That is all that matters.

Rum Runners Punch

I grew up in a time when young ladies were not allowed to go out often. As an adult, I love to go out and I particularly enjoy throwing a party. Nothing like a little punch to get a party started.

3 pints brewed tea
1 pint lemon juice
1 pint orange juice
1 cup sugar
1 pint rum
2 pints whiskey

1. Mix all the ingredients in a large punch bowl.

2. Chill and/or serve over ice.

Bloody Mary

14 ounces tomato juice
1 ounce lemon juice
1 drop Tabasco sauce
1 teaspoon Worcestershire sauce
1 ounce vodka
salt and pepper to taste

1. Mix ingredients in a large glass, add ice and shake.

2. Serve cold.

Grape Punch

Here's a non-alcoholic drink to serve, especially at kid's parties.

1 can (8 - 12 ounces) frozen grape juice
8 - 12 ounces water
1 can (8 - 12 ounces) pineapple juice
2 liters ginger ale
sliced fruit

1. Mix all ingredients in a large punch bowl. Use an empty frozen juice container to measure your water.

2. Add sliced fruit, such as, oranges, apples, pineapple, or lemons.

Pineapple Sherbet Punch

My kids love this punch. Even as adults, they say this reminds them of Sunday programs at church. I took the old recipe and gave it a few twists.

1 can (16 ounces) frozen orange juice

1 can (16 ounces) pineapple juice

2 liters ginger ale

1 pint vanilla ice cream

1/2 gallon pineapple sherbet

1. Pour the orange juice, pineapple juice, and ginger ale in a large punch bowl. Add scoops of ice cream and sherbet.

2. When serving, add liquid and scoops of ice cream to cups for your guests.

Grass Hopper Punch

Recipes don't have to be complicated. Two ingredients and you are ready go.

1/2 gallon lime sherbet

1/2 pint rum (I use Bacardi 151)

1. Scoop sherbet into punch bowl and then add rum. Mix well with a spatula or spoon.

2. Serve in small glasses or cups.

3. To look fancy, add place a mint leaf on top or hang a cut slice of lemon on the lip of the glass.

Spiced Tea

1 gallon water

4 large tea bags, steep them remove

1 small can frozen lemon juice

1 small (6 - 8 ounces) can frozen orange juice

2 cinnamon sticks

1 teaspoon whole cloves

1 cup sugar

1. In a large pot, add water and four large tea bags. Seep for two hours. You can also hot brew the tea.

2. Remove tea bags. Add lemon juice, orange juice, cinnamon, clove, and sugar.

3. Simmer for one hour.

4. Chill and serve cold.

BREADS

A word about bread

You want to be a hero? Think about coming home to the smell of hot, freshly baked bread. That'll make anyone think you're a hero.

Baking Tip

✓ When bread is baking, place a small dish of water in the oven, it helps to keep crust from getting hard.

Baking time for bread

These are the approximate timings for each stage of creating bread:

Yeast – Sugar mixture to set...5 – 15 mins
Mix butter and knead ....10 – 15 mins
First time in bulk .... 1½ hours
Folding into loaves..5 mins
Second rise (loaf pan) .... 1½ hours
Baking time ....30 – 40 mins
Cooling on rocks...30 mins

Barbecue Skillet Corn Bread

Cornbread is a Southern stable. We eat it with beans, greens, fried chicken, and almost anything else. Any southerner can make cornbread, but can you make it on a barbecue grill? This is a perfect recipe after you've grilled you meat, but your coals are still hot.

Now it gets interesting.

1/2 cup flour
2 cup corn meal
2 teaspoon baking powder
1 teaspoon sugar
1/2 teaspoon salt
1/3 cup vegetable oil
1 egg
1 1/2 cup milk
Charcoal or propane grill with a lid
Cast iron skillet

1. Heat the grill.

2. In a large bowl, stir flour, corn meal, baking powder, sugar, and salt with a spatula.

3. Mix in oil, egg, and milk.

4. Pour into a greased skillet, place on grill, and close the lid.

5. Cook until the bread is done to the touch. Depending on the heat of your grill, this could be between 20 minutes and an hour.

Fried Biscuits

I can't look at biscuits without thinking about my Uncle Robert. He was particular about his biscuits and would only eat them hot and fresh. And don't even suggest store bought biscuits.

He'd hate the idea of fried biscuits. The good news for us is that his loss is our gain.

Biscuits are great. Fried food is great. Put them together and... you be the judge.

2 cans small biscuits

2 cups oil

powdered sugar to taste

1. Heat the oil in a skillet until hot. Place the uncooked biscuits in oil one at a time.

2. Cook each biscuit for two minutes Flip over and cook until done.

3. Sprinkle with powdered sugar and serve hot.

Broccoli Corn Bread

2 packages (15 to 18 total ounces) corn muffin mix (Jiffy brand works best)

2 sticks butter, melted

4 eggs

1 cup onion, chopped

1 cup small curd cottage cheese

1 package (10 to 16 ounces) frozen chopped broccoli

1. Following the instructions on the package, cook the broccoli and drain.

2. In a large bowl, mix the muffin mix, butter, eggs, onion, cottage cheese, and broccoli.

3. Pour into a large casserole dish. Bake for at 350 degrees for 35 minutes.

Three Dollar Bill Monkey Bread

I've read quite a few monkey bread recipes. As much as I love cooking, I don't always have time to spend in kitchen. I raised kids, handled church events, family picnics, and ran a household. Sometimes, you just need a little shortcut.

Don't worry—recipe is as good as it gets.

3 cans biscuits
1/2 cup brown sugar
1/2 cup sugar
1 teaspoon cinnamon
1 cup vanilla ice cream
1 stick butter

1. In a large bowl, combine sugar, brown sugar, and cinnamon.

2. Remove biscuits from can and roll each biscuit in the sugar mix until coated.

3. Place biscuits side-by-side in a buttered bunt cake pan.

4. In a medium sauce pan, combine ice cream and butter.

5. Stirring constantly, bring to a boil. Pour over biscuits.

6. Bake at 350 degrees for 25 - 30 minutes.

7. Serve warm.

Sour Cream Corn Muffins

1 cup sour cream
2 packages (15 - 18 total ounces) corn muffin mix (Jiffy brand works best)
2 eggs
1 cup butter

1. In a large mixing bowl, combine sour cream, corn muffin mix, eggs, and butter. Pour into muffin pan.

2. Bake at 300°F for 30 minutes or until brown.

Country Rolls

2 packets dry yeast (each packet is 1/4 ounce)
2 cups lukewarm water
1 cup shortening
3/4 cup sugar
2 eggs
6 cups flour
1 teaspoon salt

1. Dissolve yeast in 1/2 cup lukewarm water and set aside.

2. In a sauce pan, melt and combine shortening and sugar.

3. In a bowl, add the shortening mixture, eggs, and salt and mix well.

4. Add the water and yeast, stir until blended.

5. Using a mixer, add flour one cup at a time until you create a dough.

6. Shape by hand into a large ball, cover with a damp towel, and set in a warm place. Allow dough to rise until doubled in size (three hours, but overnight is best).

7. Preheat oven to 350°F.

8. Grease a 9 x 13 inch pan.

9. Shape dough into three inch balls and arrange in pan.

10. With the bottom of a drinking glass, gently flatten each ball to half the height.

11. Bake for 15 minutes until golden.

Wilma's Damn Good Rolls

1 cup butter-flavored shortening

1 cup milk

2 eggs, beaten

3/4 cups sugar

1 teaspoon salt

1 cup water

2 packages yeast

1/2 cup lukewarm water for yeast

7 1/2 cups flour, sifted

1. Sprinkle yeast in 1/2 cup of lukewarm water and let sit for at least 5 minutes.

2. In a sauce pan, scald milk: bring milk almost to boiling, then remove from heat and stir in shortening.

3. In a large bowl, combine eggs and sugar until blended.

4. Add salt and 1 cup water. Stir in yeast mixture.

5. Slowly add milk, stirring.

6. Using a large mixer, blend together while add flour one cup at a time. Mix until you create dough.

7. By hand shape into a large ball, cover with a damp towel, and set in a warm place.

8. Allow to rise until the dough doubles in size (three hours, but overnight is best).

9. Grease a 9 x 13 inch pan. Shape dough into three inch balls and arrange in pan.

10. With the bottom of a drinking glass, gently flatten each ball to half the height.

11. Bake for 15 minutes until golden.

Black-eyed Pea Cornbread

If you haven't eaten black-eyed peas and cornbread, you don't know what you are missing. That's my comfort food, the kind of thing I eat after a long hard day. So, of course, one day I thought, why don't I put them together.

2 cups corn meal
1/2 teaspoon salt
1/2 teaspoon baking soda
1 cup buttermilk
1 pound pork sausage, cooked
1 can creamed corn
1 can black-eyed peas (or 1 cup fresh cooked peas)
1 small jar pimentos, chopped
green chilies
1 cup cheese, shredded
2 eggs
1/2 cup cooking oil

1. Preheat oven to 350°F. Grease a casserole pan or cast iron skillet.

2. In a large bowl, mix corn meal, salt, baking soda, buttermilk, pork sausage, peas, pimentos, oil, and chilies.

3. Add eggs & cheese while mixing until all ingredients are thoroughly blended.

4. Pour into greased pan.

5. Bake in oven for 40 minutes.

Ice Cream Muffins

So many people think cooking has to be complex. Here's a very simple recipe that will make all your friends think you are a genius.

You can always use a different flavor of ice cream.

1 1/2 cups self-rising flour
2 cups vanilla ice cream, softened

1. Preheat oven to 350°F.

2. In a large bowl, mix flour and ice cream.

3. Pour into greased muffin pan filling each slot to 3/4 full.

4. Bake for 20-25 minutes or until golden brown.

Banana Nut Bread

4 eggs
2 cups sugar
2 cups flour
2 sticks butter
1 teaspoon baking soda
1/2 teaspoons salt
3 very ripe bananas

1. In a large bowl, mix eggs, sugar, flour, butter, baking soda, salt, and bananas. Pour into two bread pan.

2. Bake at 350°F degrees for one hour.

Wilma's Southern Biscuits

Makes two dozen biscuits.

Nothing like hot biscuits first thing in the morning! Nothing like getting up at 4:00 am to make them either.

2 cups flour, sifted
4 teaspoons baking powder
1/2 teaspoon cream of tartar
1/2 teaspoon salt
2 tablespoons sugar
1/2 cup shortening, melted
1 egg beaten
2/3 cups buttermilk

1. Preheat oven to 400°F.

2. Sift the flour.

3. In a large bowl, mix flour, baking powder, salt, sugar, and cream of tartar.

4. Make a hole (indention) in the center of dry ingredients and add melted shortening, milk, and egg.

5. Stir until you make a stiff dough.

6. Remove dough from bowl and place on a floured surface, kneading about 6 times.

7. Roll or pat to ½-inch thickness.

8. Cut into pieces using a cookie cutter. Don't have a cutter? Use an upside down coffee mug.

9. Bake for about 12 minutes or until golden brown.

Newport Corn Bread

1 cup instant grits

1/2 cup flour

3 teaspoon shortening or oil

1/2 teaspoon baking powder

1/2 teaspoon salt

1 teaspoon sugar

1 cup buttermilk

1 egg

1 pound cooked sausage

1 cup shredded cheese

1. Preheat your oven at 400°F. Place a greased pan inside. I like to use a cast-iron skillet, but a casserole disk or cake pan will do.

2. In a large bowl, mix grits, flour, oil, baking powder, salt, sugar, and buttermilk until thoroughly combined.

3. Mix in milk, egg, cheese, and browned sausage.

4. Carefully, remove the pan from the oven and pour in batter.

5. Bake at 400°F for about 20 minutes.

Never Fail Roll

2 packets (each packet is 1/4 ounce) dry yeast
1 cup warm water
2 eggs
1/2 cup sugar
1 teaspoon salt
1/2 cup butter
4 1/2 cup flour

1. In a bowl, dissolve yeast in warm water.

2. Add eggs, sugar, salt, butter, and flour to yeast mixture. Stir until smooth.

3. Place in warm area, covered with towel for 3 hours or when dough rises to double in size.

4. Preheat oven to 375°F.

5. Knead the dough for 10 - 15 minutes. Shape in to rolls.

6. Place on a greased cookie sheet.

7. Bake for 20 minutes or until golden brown.

SALAD

A word about salad

I never heard the word "blue collar" until a few years ago. I was told that blue collar people work in factories, warehouses, and kitchen. Almost every job outdoors is blue collar.

I am blue collar.

Nothing wrong with that.

But it was a years later, as I tried Hawaiian food for the first time, that I really understood blue collar.

Hawaiian people eat macaroni salad.

Italians eat pasta.

Mexicans eat beans and rice.

Chinese eat rice.

Black people eat beans and corn bread.

When you're working and you're working hard, you need something that's gonna get you past that slump when you got three hours to go on a ten hour shift. When your boss asks you to stay late, only to send you home early the next day so he ain't gotta pay over time.

Salad is bunch of colorful vegetables in a bowl with a side of lemon water.

Unless you're blue collar. For us, here in the South, salad is anything you can stir into mayonnaise to get calories into you.

So this section is dedicated to anyone who's had to work on their feet and wanting nothing more at the end of the day than to just sit down.

Green Pea Salad

4 cups hard-boiled eggs

2 16 ounce cans green peas

1 medium onion, chopped

1/2 cup mayonnaise

1/2 cup sweet pickle relish

2 ounces jarred pimiento

1. In a large boil, mix eggs, peas, onion, mayonnaise, relish and pimiento.

2. Chill and serve cold.

Green Pea Salad 2

1/2 cup mayonnaise

1 teaspoon mustard

1 teaspoon vinegar

pinch salt

black pepper to taste

1 cup (or 16 ounce package) frozen green peas

1 medium onion, finely chopped

2 boiled eggs, chopped

1 teaspoon parsley

1. Thaw and drain the green peas.

2. In a medium bowl, combine mayonnaise, mustard, vinegar, salt, and pepper.

3. Add peas, onion, and eggs. Toss together and sprinkle to parsley.

4. Chill before serving.

Fruit Dressing

Every time I serve this, I get the same questions: What is this? What's fruit dressing?

You heard of salad dressing? Well, this is the same thing...except for fruit, I answer. By that time, they're too busy eating to pay me no mind.

1 3-ounce package cream cheese

2 teaspoons honey

1 1/2 tablespoon lemon juice

pinch salt

pinch cayenne pepper

1/4 cup vegetable oil

1. In a large bowl, mix cream cheese, honey, lemon juice, salt, cayenne pepper and oil. Mix well and chill.

2. Serve over your favorite fruit.

Chicken Salad

2 cans white chicken

1/2 cup chopped celery

3/4 cup nuts chopped - I use pecans or walnuts

1 apple (sour or sweet depending on your preference)

mayonnaise to taste

1. Skin, core, and cube an apple.

2. In a medium bowl, mix chicken, celery, and apple.

3. Add mayonnaise a tablespoon at a time until you have a consistency you enjoy.

4. Chill and serve over lettuce or in a sandwich. You can also scoop out a tomato for that extra fancy touch.

Ranch Chicken Salad

2 cups cooked chicken, cubed

1 cup chopped celery

1 can (20-ounces) crushed pineapple

1/4 cup pineapple juice

1 package ranch dressing mix

1/2 cup mayonnaise

1. Drain the can of pineapple and set the juice aside.

2. In a large bowl, combine chicken, celery, and pineapple. Add dressing mix and chicken. Stir well.

3. Chill before serving with bread or crackers.

Homemade Cold Slaw

1 medium cabbage head, finely chopped

1 medium onion, chopped

1/2 cup cooking oil

1/2 cup sugar

1 teaspoon celery seeds

1. In a bowl, combine cabbage, onion, oil, sugar, and celery seeds. Mix well using a spoon or by hand.

2. Chill before serving.

Broccoli Salad

1 bunch broccoli
1 head cauliflower
3 to 4 stalks of celery
1 small red onion
1 red pepper
1/2 cup ranch dressing

1. Chop the broccoli, cauliflower, celery, onion, and pepper finely.

2. Mix in a bowl with ranch dressing.

Broccoli Coleslaw

Here's another simple, but necessary recipe. You can't have barbecue without some kind of coleslaw.

I mean, really.

1 package (16 ounces or so) broccoli
3/4 cup apple cider vinegar
3/4 cup sugar
3/4 cup canola or vegetable oil

1. Chop broccoli into bite-sized pieces.

2. In a large bowl, combine broccoli, vinegar, sugar, and oil. Mix well.

3. Chill and served cold.

Old Time Potato Salad

6 potatoes (yellow or red)

1 cup of mayonnaise

1 teaspoon salt

2 tablespoon vinegar

1 teaspoon pepper

1/2 cup onion, chopped

1 cup celery, chopped

6 hard-boiled eggs

1/2 cup pickled radish

1 small jar pimento

1. Clean your potatoes. You can skin them if you like. Boil or microwave potatoes until they are cooked but still firm. Let cool.

2. Peel and cut the eggs into chunks.

3. In a large bowl, mix mayonnaise, salt, vinegar, pepper, onion, celery, eggs, picked radish, and pimento.

4. Add potatoes and mix well.

5. Serve chilled.

Pasta Salad

There is a great debate about which pasta to use for pasta salad. I like elbow macaroni. Other people like bow tie. Some that like elbow macaroni like the large ones—I like the small ones.

This is my cookbook so my recipe uses small elbow macaroni.

One pound package pasta - I use elbow macaroni
1 package dry Italian dressing mix
2 bottles Italian dressing
1 cup cucumber, diced
1 cup yellow squash, diced
1 cup zucchini, diced
2 cups tomatoes, diced
1 cup black olives
2 small cans small shrimp
1¼ cup vinegar

1. Boil pasta. Drain and set aside.

2. In a large bowl, combine cucumber, squash, zucchini, tomatoes, and olives.

3. Add dressing, dressing mix, and vinegar.

4. Toss with shrimp and pasta.

Chicken and Avocado Salad

3 cups chicken, diced
½ cup celery, diced
1 cup black olive, sliced
½ cup mayonnaise
1½ cup avocado, diced
1 teaspoon lemon juice
dash cayenne pepper

1. Blend chicken, celery, and olives with mayonnaise.

2. Add lemon juice and cayenne pepper. You can also salt and pepper to taste.

3. Chill and add Avocado just before serving.

VEGETABLES

A word about vegetables

Vegetable don't have to be boring. Dock'em up!

Vegetable Tips

- ✓ To keep green vegetables brightly colored, add 1/8 teaspoon salt to the cooking water.
- ✓ Never refrigerate tomatoes; cold kills the flavor.
- ✓ While cooking vegetables that will give off an unpleasant odor, simmer a small pan of vinegar on top of stove.
- ✓ Two things to do to keep cabbage smell from filling the kitchen: I don't oven cook it and I put 1/2 a lemon in the water boiling it.
- ✓ To avoid tears when peeling an onion, peel onion under cold water, or refrigerate before chopping.
- ✓ To hurry up baked potatoes boil in salty water for 10 minutes, then place in a very hot oven, this will cut the bake time shorter.
- ✓ Mash potatoes use a couple of teaspoons of cream cheese in place of butter.
- ✓ Dampen a paper towel or terry cloth and brush downward on the corn cob, every corn silk strand should come off.
- ✓ Keep tomatoes in storage with stem pointing downward, they will retain their freshness longer.
- ✓ Sunlight doesn't ripen tomatoes, it's the warmth that makes them ripe. So find a warm spot near the stove or dishwasher where they can get a little heat.
- ✓ Save the juice from canned tomatoes in ice cube tray. When frozen, store in a plastic bag in freezer for cooking or use in tomato drinks.
- ✓ If fresh vegetables are welted or blemished, pick off the brown edges. Sprinkle with cool water, wrap in paper towel and refrigerate for an hour or so.
- ✓ "Pick up crispy lettuce, adding lemon juice to a bowl of cold water, add lettuce and refrigerate for an hour or so.
- ✓ Lettuce and celery will crisp up first if you place in a pan of cool water, add lemon juice, add a few potatoes, and refrigerate for an hour or so. "

- ✓ By lining the crisper section of your refrigerator with newspaper and wrapping vegetables with it, moisture will be absorbed, and your vegetables will stay fresh longer.
- ✓ Store leftover corn, peas, green beans, carrots or any vegetable in a container in the freezer, add to soup or stew.
- ✓ Onion, broccoli, and Brussel sprouts will cook faster if you make an x-shaped cut o the base of the vegetable.
- ✓ Do not store potatoes in the refrigerator, the starch will convert to sugar, changing the flavor.
- ✓ To cut down on the odor when cooking cabbage and other vegetable cauliflower, add a litter of water and boil on the side.

Greens

Later in life, I was able to travel to other parts of the US and the world. Everyone one has their home food. You know, the thing that everyone eats in your neighborhood.

We have so many home foods, it is hard to agree on one, but if I had to choose a single food, I'd have to choose greens.

Greens come in many forms. The most common that we eat are: mustard, turnip, and collard.

Mustard greens are the least bitter (I want to say sweetest, but my editor tells me that "sweet" and "not bitter" are two different things.

Turnip greens are the best value. You can buy turnips with stalks and have both turnips and greens for dinner.

Collards are bitter and tough, but oh, so good.

2 - 3 pounds of greens of your choice, mix if you like

2 ham hocks, 1/2 pound of salt pork, or two smoked turkey necks

1. In a large pot, boil meat for 45 minutes.

2. While the meat is cooking, wash greens with cool water. Do this 2 or 3 times to remove dirt, and grit.

3. Chop your greens into pieces that can be eaten with a fork. To do this, you can use a knife on a cutting board, cut with kitchen scissors, or tear by hand.

4. Place greens in hot water with meat. Cover pot and cook for 30 minutes.

Mixed Greens

I don't mess around with greens!

3 - 4 pounds of mixed greens, for example turnip greens, kale, spinach, collard greens, or mustard greens
3 cups water
½ teaspoon black pepper
3 bouillon cubes (chicken, pork, or beef)
3 tablespoons vinegar
1 tablespoon allspice

1. Wash greens, removing dirt and grit.

2. Cut greens into pieces that be eaten with a fork.

3. Put water in a large pot and bring to a boil.

4. Add greens, pepper, bouillon cubes, vinegar, and allspice.

5. Cover pot and boil until greens are tender. About 2 hours.

Baked Beans

30 ounces pork 'n beans
1 cup ketchup
1/2 cup brown sugar
1/4 cup maple syrup
1 medium onion, chopped
1 pound smoked sausage
1 teaspoon liquid smoke
1 tablespoon Worcester sauce

1. Preheat oven to 350°F.

2. In a large bowl, mix pork 'n beans, ketchup, sugar, syrup, onion, sausage, liquid smoke, and Worcestershire sauce.

3. Pour into dish (I use a cast iron skillet). Bake for one hour.

Fried Green Beans

2 cups flour
6 teaspoon baking powder
1 teaspoon salt
3 eggs
1 cup milk
1 pound whole green beans
1/2 teaspoon black pepper
1/2 teaspoon red pepper

1. Sift flour, baking powder, and salt to make a flour mixture.

2. In a separate bowl, combine eggs and milk.

3. Add the flour mixture. Stir until smooth.

4. Add fresh green beans and stir with spoon.

5. Heat three tablespoons of oil in a skillet over medium heat.

6. Sauté green beans until the beans are crisp.

Baked Acorn Squash

3 medium acorn squash
1/2 cup butter
salt
6 teaspoon cooking wine
nutmeg
2 teaspoon brown sugar

1. Preheat oven at 350°F degrees.

2. Wash squash and cut in half length-wise. Place in baking dish.

3. Rub the inside of squash with butter. Sprinkle each squash with salt, nutmeg, and sugar. Drizzle with cooking wine.

4. Bake for 50 minutes.

Old Time Fried Corn

This is the next best thing to eating the corn off the cob.

1 can whole kernel corn
1 can cream style corn
1/3 cup vegetable oil
1 tablespoon flour
1/2 cup butter

1. Heat oil in skillet.

2. When hot, add whole kernel corn and creamed corn.

3. Add butter, lower heat, and cover. Simmer for 20 minutes.

4. Stir in flour to thicken, replace cover and simmer another 20 - 30 minutes.

Fried Corn

1 can (12 ounces) creamed corn
1 can (4 ounces) whole corn
1/4 cup vegetable oil
1/2 teaspoon crushed red pepper
1/2 teaspoon black pepper
1 tablespoon all-purpose flour
1 tablespoon butter

1. Heat oil in pan or skillet.

2. Add whole corn, creamed corn, red pepper, black pepper. Simmer over low heat for 20 minutes.

3. Add flour and cook for 5 additional minutes.

4. Top with butter.

Marinade for Vegetables

Marinades aren't just for meat! I marinade my vegetables before grilling or baking all the time. This adds an incredible amount of flavor.

1 cucumber

1 small onion

1 tomato

1/3 cup vinegar

1/3 cup water

1 tablespoon sugar

1 teaspoon salt

1 jalapeno or other hot pepper (optional)

1. Dice cucumber, onion, and tomato and place in a bowl or sealable bag.

2. Add vinegar, water, sugar, and salt. Stir ingredients together. Add pepper if you like a kick to your veggies.

Marinating your vegetables

Here's list of vegetables you can soak in the marinade before grilling or baking:

- ✓ Asparagus
- ✓ Bell peppers
- ✓ Corn
- ✓ Eggplant
- ✓ Mushrooms
- ✓ Okra
- ✓ Onions
- ✓ Peppers and chilies
- ✓ Potatoes
- ✓ Snap peas
- ✓ Squash
- ✓ Tomato
- ✓ Zucchini

Wrapped Green Beans

2 pounds fresh green beans,

  2 pounds frozen green beans (thawed), or

  2 cans (16 ounces each) green beans

1 pound sliced bacon (uncooked)

toothpicks

1. Preheat oven to 375•F.

2. Cut each slice of uncooked bacon in half.

3. If you are using canned green beans, open and drain each can.

4. Wrap a small bunch (3 - 4) green beans in bacon. Secure with a toothpick at each end and place on a baking sheet or in a pan.

5. Bake until bacon is crisp.

The Very Best Fried Green Tomatoes

1 cup flour
1 cup cornmeal
1 teaspoon salt
1 teaspoon pepper
1 teaspoon sugar
3 green tomatoes (unpeeled)
1 cup buttermilk

1. Cut tomatoes into slices.

2. In a medium bowl, make batter by mixing flour, cornmeal, salt, pepper, sugar, and buttermilk.

3. Dip tomato slices into batter.

4. In a pan or skillet, heat vegetable oil.

5. Fry tomato slices until each side is crispy.

6. Drain on paper towels. Serve hot.

CASSEROLES

A word about casseroles

It's the end of a long day of work. The last thing you want to do is stand over a hot stove, but dinner needs to be made.

Sometimes, a casserole is the way to go.

Casseroles are tasty. The ingredients are simple. You can easily add vegetables for finicky kids and picky eaters.

And best part, you throw the ingredients in and walk away for half an hour or so.

Even the end of the day brings dozens of things you need to do. Get the casserole going and get through that to do list.

Or get off your feet. Either works.

Cousin Oliver Rice

1 cup rice, uncooked
1 envelope (4 ounces) vegetable soup mix
1 can (6 - 10 ounces) cream of mushroom soup
1/2 cup butter
3 cups water

1. In a skillet, melt butter and stir in rice.

2. Cook over low heat for five minutes.

3. Mix in water, soup, and soup mix. Cover and boil for 20 - 30 minutes.

Arkansas Hash

1 pound ground beef
1 tablespoon chili powder
1/2 teaspoon salt
1/2 cup onion
1/2 cup bell pepper
1/2 cup celery
1 can (6 - 8 ounces) stewed tomatoes
1/2 cup uncooked rice
1 clove garlic
1 medium can tomato sauce
1 cup water

1. Over medium heat, brown ground beef in skillet with salt and chili powder.

2. Add onion, bell pepper, celery, stewed tomatoes, rice, garlic, tomato sauce, and water. Cover and cook for 45 minutes.

Taco Dinner

2 pounds ground beef
1 onion, chopped
1 green pepper, chopped
1 can (6 - 8 ounces) stewed tomatoes
8 ounces grated cheese
1 large bag corn chips (I like flavored corn chips)
2 tomatoes, chopped
1/2 head lettuce, chopped

1. Cook ground beef.

2. As the beef browns, add salt, onion, green pepper, and stewed tomatoes.

3. Preheat oven to 355°F.

4. Crush bag of corn chips until the pieces are very fine and cover the bottom of a baking dish.

5. Pour meat mixture over chips and top with cheese.

6. Bake for 30 minutes.

7. Cool and top with lettuce and tomatoes.

Tuna Casserole

1/3 cup onion, diced
1 tablespoon margarine
1 small can tuna
1 can cream mushroom soup
1/2 cup milk
2 cups uncooked noodles - spaghetti noodles will work
1 cup American cheese, diced
1 cup potato chips, crushed

1. Preheat oven to 350°F.

2. In a pan or skillet, cook onion in margarine.

3. Stir in soup and add milk until all ingredients are blended well.

4. Bring to a simmer for 2 minutes.

5. Stir in tuna and noodles and heat for another 2 minutes.

6. Pour ingredients in baking dish and top with crushed potato chips.

7. Bake at for 30 minutes.

Potatoes Au Gratin

5 medium potatoes, sliced and cooked
1/2 stick margarine
2 tablespoons flour
1 teaspoon salt
1/2 teaspoon pepper
1 cup milk
1 cup cheddar cheese, grated
1/2 cup cracker crumbs

1. Preheat oven 350°F.

2. Arrange potatoes in a greased casserole dish.

3. In a saucepan, combine margarine, flour, salt, pepper, and milk.

4. Heat and add cheese until melted.

5. Pour sauce over potatoes. Top with cracker crumbs.

6. Bake for 30 minutes.

Cornbread Casserole

2 1/2 cups cornmeal
1/2 cup flour
1/2 teaspoon salt
1/2 teaspoon baking soda
2 teaspoon baking powder
2 eggs
1 medium onion, chopped
1 medium green bell pepper, chopped
3 celery stalks, chopped
18 ounces cheddar cheese, grated
18 ounces Colby cheese, grated
1 cup buttermilk
1/2 cup oil
3 cups chicken broth

1. Preheat oven to 350°F.

2. In a large bowl, combine cornmeal, flour, salt, baking soda, baking powder.

3. Add milk, chicken broth, eggs, onion, bell pepper, and celery.

4. Stir in cheese and oil.

5. Pour into a large casserole dish.

6. Place a large pan in the oven and bake casserole on pan for 1 hour.

Best Breakfast Casserole

4 eggs

1/3 cup milk

4 cups frozen shredded hash browns - can substitute fried, chopped
potatoes

1/3 cup butter

1/2 pounds chopped ham

1 cups shredded cheese

salt and pepper to taste

1. Preheat oven to 350°F.

2. Place hash browns in casserole dish.

3. In a large bowl, crack eggs and beat with a fork while adding milk.

4. Stir in butter, ham, and cheese.

5. Pour mixture in casserole dish.

6. Cover and bake for 45 minutes.

Rice and Broccoli Casserole

1 1/2 cups rice, cooked

1 can (8 ounces) cream of broccoli soup

1 can (8 ounces) cream of mushroom soup

1 can (8 ounces) cream of chicken soup

1 cup grated cheese (American, cheddar, or nacho)

1. Preheat oven to 350°F.

2. In medium bowl, mix soups and rice.

3. Pour into casserole dish. Top with cheese.

4. Cover and bake for 20 minutes.

Eggplant Casserole

1 large eggplant

3 eggs

½ cup flour

1 cup milk

vegetable oil frying

salt and pepper to taste

1 clove garlic, chopped

1 teaspoon allspice seasoning

2 bell peppers, chopped

2 medium onions, chopped

1 cup bread crumbs

2 tomatoes, sliced

2 cups mozzarella cheese, diced

1. Preheat oven to 350°F.

2. Cut eggplant into slices 3/8 inches thick.

3. Cut unpeeled eggplant, slice 3/8 thick. In a skillet or pan, fry on each side until golden brown.

4. In a large casserole dish, layer eggplant, bell pepper, onion, tomatoes, cheese, and bread crumbs.

5. In a separate bowl, beat eggs and add milk. Pour into casserole dish.

6. Bake for 45 minutes.

7. Let stand for 10 minutes before serving.

MEAT AND ENTRIES

Meat Tips

- ✓ To reheat roast, wrap on aluminum foil and heat on low.
- ✓ Seal the meat in a plastic bag and place in a bowl of very warm water or put it in a bag and let cool water run over it for an hour.
- ✓ Poke a hole in the middle of the patty while shaping the burger. The burger will cook faster and the hole will disappear when done.
- ✓ To tenderize tough meat, boil with a teaspoon of vinegar in the cooking water.
- ✓ Tough meat or game meat, make a marinade of equal parts cooking oil, vinegar, bouillon, heated and marinated for two hours.
- ✓ Chicken to stew and old hen: soak it in vinegar for several hours before cooking and it will taste like a spring chicken.
- ✓ Roll a package of bacon into a tube before opening, this loosens the slices and keeps them from sticking.
- ✓ For golden brown chicken, roll in powdered milk instead of flour.
- ✓ Try using crushed cornflakes or cornbread instead of bread crumbs. This will give the meatball a different onion flavor, this is also good for meatloaf.
- ✓ Boil hot dog in sweet pickle juice and a little water for a different taste.

Beef Brisket

5 - 6 pound brisket
8 ounces barbecue sauce
1 teaspoon celery salt
1 teaspoon garlic powder
1 teaspoon onion powder
3 ounces liquid smoke
1/2 cup water
1 cup Worcestershire sauce
salt and pepper to taste

1. Wash brisket and place in large baking pan.

2. Sprinkle with liquid smoke and then season with salt, celery salt, onion powder, and garlic powder.

3. Cover with aluminum foil. Set brisket in refrigerator overnight.

4. Preheat oven at 275°F.

5. Cook brisket for 5 hours.

6. Remove foil, cover the meat with barbecue sauce, and then replace foil and bake for another hour.

Sausage Balls

1 pound pork sausage
1/2 pound cheddar cheese
3 cups all-purpose flour - I use Bisquick brand.

1. Preheat oven to 400°F.

2. In a large bowl, hand mix sausage, cheese, and flour.

3. Form into balls and bake for 15 minutes.

Forgotten Chicken

1/2 pound mushroom
2 tablespoons butter
2 cans (8 ounces each) cream of mushroom soup
1 can evaporated milk
1 cup rice
1/2 package onion soup mix
1 chicken, cut up, uncooked

1. Preheat oven to 350°F.

2. In a pan or skillet, sauté mushrooms in butter.

3. In a large bowl, combine mushrooms, soup, milk, rice, and soup mix. Pour mixture in casserole dish.

4. Place chicken on top. Do not stack the pieces.

5. Cover and bake for 2 hours. No peeking.

Oven fried chicken

1 whole chicken
1 teaspoon paprika
salt and pepper to taste
1/2 cup all-purpose flour
1/2 cup butter

1. Preheat oven to 375°F degrees.

2. Thaw (if necessary) and cut up one chicken.

3. Salt and pepper chicken to taste.

4. Roll chicken in flour.

5. Place chicken pieces in a pan and bake 1 1/2 hours or until done.

Sloppy Joe

1 1/2 pounds ground beef
1 medium onion, chopped
3/4 cup ketchup
1/3 cup sweet pickle relish
1 tablespoon brown sugar
1 tablespoon mustard
1 teaspoon chili powder
1/2 teaspoon salt
1/2 teaspoon black pepper
8 buns

1. In a large pan or skillet, brown ground beef with onion.

2. When the meat is cooked, add ketchup, relish, sugar, mustard, chili powder, salt, and pepper. Simmer until you reach the desired thickness.

3. Serve on buns.

Barbecue Chicken

1 whole chicken
1 stick margarine
salt and pepper
1 bottle barbecue sauce

1. Preheat oven to 350°F.

2. Season chicken with salt and pepper.

3. Arrange chicken on a 9 x 13-inch pan.

4. Place a pat margarine on each piece of chicken.

5. Cover with barbecue sauce and a lid of aluminum foil.

6. Bake in oven for 1 hour.

Italian Grilled Cheese Sandwiches

For each sandwich, use the following:

2 slices of bread - I use white bread
mayonnaise
2 slices cheese (American, cheddar, or your favorite)
1 - 2 slices tomato
basil
oregano
butter

1. Spread mayonnaise on each slice of bread and sprinkle with basil and oregano.

2. Make a sandwich with cheese and tomato slices.

3. In a pan or skillet, heat butter.

4. Place sandwich in pan until one side forms a crust.

5. Flip over and grill the other side, adding butter as needed.

6. Remove when both sides have formed a tasty crust and cheese is melted.

Pot Roast Beef with Vegetable

8 - 10 pound beef pot roast
¼ cups flour
1 teaspoon black pepper
¾ teaspoon salt
¼ cups oil
5 small onions, quartered
8 small carrots, cut into bite size pieces
8 small potatoes
½ cup water
5 peppercorns
3 bay leaves

1. Mix flour, salt, pepper, and rub on roast to season.

2. Heat oil in a heavy skillet or Dutch oven. Add roast and cook over medium heat, turning to brown on all sides.

3. Add potatoes, water, pepper corns, and bay leaves. Cook over medium heat for 2 hours.

4. Add onions and carrots. Cook 30 minutes or until vegetables are tender.

5. Skim excess fat. Remove bay leaf and pepper corns.

6. Serve on a platter with vegetables.

Want gravy?
1 tablespoon flour
1 tablespoon corn starch
juice from cooked roast

1. In a pan or skillet, heat 1/4 to 1/2 cup of juice from the roast.

2. Add 1 tablespoon flour and 1 tablespoon corn starch.

3. Cook until thick.

Meat Loaf

1 pound ground beef

1 teaspoon salt

½ teaspoon pepper

2 cup bread crumb

1/3 cup Lea & Perrins Traditional Steak Sauce

2 cups milk

tomato soup

2 eggs

1 small onion, chopped

1. Preheat oven to 350°F.

2. In a large bowl, mix ground beef, salt, pepper, bread crumbs, milk, eggs, and onion. I mix it by hand.

3. Form into a loaf, bake for 1 hour.

4. Let stand for 5 minutes and cut into slices.

Fried Baloney and Cheese Sandwich

Sometimes the simplest things are the yummiest

3 slices bologna (at least 1/8 inch thick)

2 slices cheese (American, cheddar, or whatever your favorite)

2 pats butter

2 slices of bread

1. In a pan or skillet, fry baloney in hot oil until brown around edges. Butter slices of bread.

2. Make a sandwich with bologna and cheese. Fry until brown on both sides.

Branch High "64" Fried Chicken

This recipe took me years to perfect. I'd put it against anyone's fried chicken.

You might not get it right the first time. Frying chicken is art and science. It takes a little work to get the timing right.

2½ to 3 pounds of chicken parts (legs, thighs, breasts, and/or wings)
¼ teaspoon pepper
3 cups water
1 cup flour
1 tablespoon salt
oil for frying
2 teaspoon fine herbs
2 teaspoon onion powder
2 envelopes instant chicken broth
2 teaspoon seasoned salt

1. Place chicken in a medium bowl. Cover with water and salt and chill in refrigerator for one hour.

2. In an electric blender, mix fine herbs, onion powder, seasoned salt, instant chicken broth, and pepper. Pour into a paper bag. Add flour.

3. Remove chicken from water and let it drain.

4. Shake 2 - 3 pieces at a time in the bag until covered with flour.

5. In a pan or skillet, using medium high heat enough oil to cover chicken. Remember, the oil will rise as you put chicken in.

6. Fry chicken until each side is brown and the middle is cooked.

Pork Neck Bones

We that live in the South love neck bones anyway you want to mix it up. If you don't see neck bones at your grocery store, have a conversation with your local butcher.

3 or more pounds pork neck bones

salt

pepper

garlic powder

barbecue sauce

1. Wash neck bones and season to taste.

2. On a hot grill, cook for 1 to 2 hours.

3. Remove from grill, place in large aluminum pan.

4. Preheat oven to 350°F.

5. Cover bones with barbecue sauce. Bake for 1 hour.

Easy Pork Chops

6 pork chops

1 can cream-style corn

½ cup milk

salt and pepper to taste

1. Preheat oven to 325°F.

2. Season pork chops with salt and pepper and place in a pan or casserole dish.

3. Cover with corn and milk.

4. Bake for 1 hour or until tender.

Chicken for Dumplings

1 whole chicken
salt
black pepper
garlic powder
½ cup celery, chopped
½ cup onion
1 cup green peas
1 tablespoon poultry seasoning

1. Season the chicken with salt, pepper, and garlic powder.

2. In a large pot, boil chicken in water until tender (about an hour).

3. Debone chicken, remove skin, and dice meat. Return to pot.

4. Add celery, onion, peas, and seasoning. Cook until tender.

5. Drop in dumplings and cook until dumplings are tender.

Never Fail Dumpling

Here's simple dumplings to add to your soups or stews. After working on your feet all day, there's nothing like a bowl of dumplings for dinner.

1 1/2 cups flour
1/2 teaspoon salt
3 teaspoons shortening
1 egg
5 tablespoons chicken broth

1. In a large bowl, mix flour, salt, and shortening.

2. Add broth and egg. Stir until you make a soft dough.

3. Divide into two parts, roll until flat and allow to dry for 15 minutes.

4. Cut into small strips, about the size of a dumpling.

5. Add to broth, soup, or stew. Cook until tender.

La Tonya's Chicken N Dumpling

I lost both my daughter and father-in-law in the same year. My father-in-law loved my La Tonya's chicken and dumpling. I will always remember the joy it brought them both.

This recipe is for them.

2 cups flour
½ tablespoon salt
4 tablespoons shortening
1 egg
8 tablespoons chicken broth

1. In a large bowl, mix flour and salt.

2. Add shortening, an egg, and chicken broth.

3. Make a soft dough, divide into two parts, and roll out very thin sheet.

4. Cut into small strips, drop into boiling broth. Cook until tender.

Grilled Streak

3 pounds steak (1 1/2 inches thick) - use your favorite cut
1 tablespoon garlic powder
salt and pepper to taste
2 tablespoons hot sauce - I like Louisiana brand hot sauce

5. Wash and rub meat generously on both sides with garlic, salt pepper and hot sauce. The hot sauce helps to tenderize the steak, giving it flavor. The brand I use doesn't make the flavor too hot.

6. Let sit 20 to 30 minutes before cooking.

7. Use tongs when handling the steak. A fork will allow the juice and flavor to leak out.

8. On a hot grill, cook 4 min on one side and 3 on the other. If you like it well done you can cook more.

Pork Chop with Sauerkraut

6 thick pork chops
1 cup flour
2 teaspoon garlic salt
2 teaspoons black pepper
vegetable oil
1 can (16 ounces) sauerkraut
1 cup water

1. Sprinkle pork chops with garlic salt and pepper

2. Roll in flour.

3. In a pan or skillet, heat oil over medium.

4. When oil is hot, fry chops until brown on both sides.

5. Preheat oven to 350°F.

6. Rinse kraut well in colander and place in a baking dish. Add water and place chops on top.

7. Bake for 1½ hours.

Grilled Ribeye or T-bone steak

2 - 3 steaks
2 teaspoons olive oil per steak
salt and pepper

1. Rub each steak with olive oil. Season with salt and pepper. Chill 2 to 24 hours.

2. Place on hot grill and cook until you get the level of "done" you desire.

Sunday Baked Chicken

1 large chicken
1 stick margarine
1 tablespoon parsley, chopped
1 teaspoon salt
1 teaspoon pepper
½ teaspoon thyme
½ teaspoon sage
1 clove garlic, diced
1 apple, sliced
1 onion, chopped
1 cup celery, chopped

1. Preheat oven to 350°F.

2. Loosen skin around the neck of chicken.

3. In a pan, combine margarine, parsley, salt, pepper, thyme, sage and garlic. Heat to make a paste.

4. Rub paste on the outside of the chicken and under the skin.

5. Stuff cavity of chicken with onions, apple, and celery.

6. Bake in oven for one hour.

Turkey in the Sack

1 turkey (14 to 16 pound)

1 cup of hot water

1 teaspoon black pepper

1 teaspoon salt

3 teaspoon paprika

1 tablespoon onion powder

1 teaspoon garlic powder

1 cup vegetable oil

1. Preheat oven to 325°F.

2. To make a seasoning mix, combine pepper, salt, paprika, onion powder, garlic powder, and hot water in a bowl. Let stand for 10 minutes.

3. Add oil and mix well.

4. Turkeys come with a pack of the organs and neck stuff in the middle. Remove this. You can use it for gravy.

5. Wash turkey well. Rub season mix over turkey and inside. Place turkey inside brown paper sack and put in a large roasting pan.

6. Use aluminum foil to hold the bag closed. You don't have to do anything fancy. Fold the end of the bag down and using a sheet of foil to crimp the bag closed.

7. Bake in oven 10 minutes per pound. A 15 pound turkey will take 150 minutes, or 2 hours and 30 minutes.

No Bake Meat Loaf

1 can (8 ounces) tomato soup
1 roll salted crackers
1½ pound ground beef
1 teaspoon salt
1 egg
pepper to taste
1 medium onion, finely chopped
3 tablespoons vegetable oil

1. In a bowl, mix ½ can soup with crackers, beef, salt, egg, pepper, and onion. Shape into a loaf.

2. In a pan or skillet, heat oil. Brown on load of both sides.

3. Cover and let it cook for 25 minutes.

4. Remove liquid and add remaining soup. Cook uncovered 20 minutes.

Quick and Easy Mac & Cheese

8 ounces macaroni, cooked
8 ounces shredded cheddar cheese
1 can (8 - 10 ounces) cream of mushroom soup
1/2 cup whole or 2% milk - I use PET brand milk

5. Preheat oven to 375°F.

6. In a bowl, mix macaroni, cheese, and soup. While stirring, add milk.

7. Pour in a baking dish and cook in oven for 20 - 30 minutes.

Cream of Salmon Loaf

1 can salmon
1 cup corn meal
1 small onion, chopped
½ cup bread crumbs
2 eggs
1/3 cup celery
1/8 tablespoon black pepper
½ teaspoon salt
6 tablespoons oil
1 can cream of mushroom soup

1. Preheat oven to 350°F.

2. To flake your salmon, run a fork along the edge of each piece to find and remove any bones.

3. In a bowl, combine salmon, onion, bread crumbs, eggs, celery, salt, and pepper. Form into a loaf and roll in corn meal.

4. In a pan or skillet, heat oil and fry until brown on both sides.

5. Add one can of cream of mushroom and one can of water.

6. Remove from skillet and place in baking dish.

7. Bake for 30 minutes.

Salisbury Loaf

2 eggs

1/4 cup parsley, chopped

1 cup milk

1/4 cup onion, chopped

1 teaspoon salt

1 1/2 pounds ground beef

1/2 teaspoon black pepper

1 tablespoon Worcestershire sauce

4 cups corn flakes, crushed - use the unfrosted variety

1. Preheat oven to 350°F.

2. In a large bowl, mix beef, eggs, parsley, milk, onion, salt, pepper, and Worcestershire sauce.

3. Add corn flakes and mix thoroughly.

4. Shape into a loaf and place in a loaf pan.

5. Bake for 45 – 50 minutes.

DESSERTS

Dessert Tips

- ✓ You can cut a meringue pie cleanly by coating both sides of the knife lightly with butter.
- ✓ To get more juice from lemons or oranges, quickly heat them with water for several minutes before squeezing.
- ✓ Let egg whites stand at room temperature for an hour before beating them and they will have better volume.
- ✓ To ripen green pears just place 2 or 3 in a brown bag loosely closed and at room temperature out of direct sunlight.
- ✓ To make an inexpensive syrup for pancakes, save a small amount of leftover jams and jellies in a jar. You can make a fruit-flavored syrup by adding 2 cups of sugar and a cup of fruit juice and boiling.
- ✓ A quick way to whip cream cheese: add a pinch of salt to the cream cheese before whipping, strengthening the fat cells and making them more elastic so the cream cheese will stiffen much more quickly.
- ✓ Before measuring honey or syrup, oil up the cup with cooking oil, then rinse with hot water.
- ✓ An ice cream scoop can be used to fill cupcake paper — this will help you not spill batter.
- ✓ Add a slice of soft bread to the package of brown sugar, close the bag tightly, and in a few hours the brown sugar will be soft again.
- ✓ You can also place a slice of apple in your brown sugar and it will keep the sugar from drying out and lumping.
- ✓ If you need it in a hurry, simply grate the amount of brown sugar called for with a hand grater.

Fruit Salad

1 large can (at least 12 ounces) fruit cocktail or
       2 cups chopped fruit
2 cups miniature marshmallows
1 teaspoon lemon juice
whipped cream
grated lemon peel (*optional*)
nuts for topping (*optional*)

1. Combine fruit cocktail and marshmallows, and let set in refrigerator for about 1 hour.

2. Drain excess liquid, add lemon juice and grated peel.

3. When serving, top with whipped cream and nuts.

Potato Chip Cookies

Yes, you read that right. Cookies and potato chips. Trust me. The cookies are great.

2 cups flour
1 cup shortening
1 cup brown sugar
1 cup white sugar
1 teaspoon baking soda
2 eggs
2 cups potato chips, crushed
6-ounce package chocolate chip or butterscotch chips

1. Preheat oven at 325°F.

2. In a large bowl, combine flour, shortening, brown sugar, white sugar, and eggs. Mix well.

3. Mix in crushed potato chips and chocolate chips.

4. Roll into balls about the size of a walnut. Place on cookie sheet and bake for 10 - 12 minutes.

Meringue Surprise

2 egg whites
1 teaspoon vanilla
1/8 teaspoon salt
1/2 cup sugar
1 package (6 ounces) chocolate chips
1/4 teaspoon cream of tartar

1. Preheat oven to 300°F .

2. Combine egg whites, vanilla, and salt. Beat until stiff.

3. Add sugar and tartar. Continuing beating until stiff.

4. Gently fold in chocolate chips.

5. Using a tablespoon or your finger, drop dough on cookie sheet.

6. Bake in oven for 30 minutes.

Easy Cookies

1 stick butter (1/2 a cup)
16 - 20 graham crackers, crushed
1 cup chocolate chips
1 cup coconut, shredded
1 cup pecan, chopped
1 can (14 ounces) sweetened condensed milk

1. In a pan, melt 1 stick of butter and pour on to 11 x 14 cookie sheet.

2. Layer cookie sheet with crushed graham cracker. Liberally sprinkle on chocolate chips, coconut, and nuts.

3. Pour condensed milk on top.

4. Bake at 350 degrees for 20 minutes.

Special Choco Cookies

1 package chocolate cake mix

2 package instant pudding mix

1 egg

1 cup vegetable oil

1 cup pecans (your favorite nut will work)

1. Preheat oven to 325°F.

2. In a large bowl, combine the cake mix and pudding mix. Stir in egg, oil, and nuts.

3. Use a spoon to drop batter on ungreased cookie sheet.

4. Bake in oven for one hour.

Dessert Turtles

1 package (12 ounces) chocolate chips

1 package (12 ounces) butterscotch chips

1 package (16 ounces) peanuts (shelled and salted)

1. In a microwavable bowl, partially melt chocolate in microwave. Add butterscotch chips and completely melt in microwave.

2. Add peanuts and mix well.

3. Drop teaspoon-sized pieces on cookie sheet.

4. Place in freezer until hardened. Remove and store in airtight container.

Best Ever Sugar Cookies

1 cup sugar

1 cup butter

1 teaspoon vanilla

dash salt

1 egg

2 ½ cups flour

½ teaspoon baking soda

¼ teaspoon nutmeg

1. In a large bowl, stir sugar and butter until well blended and mix in egg.

2. In a separate bowl, blend together flour, baking soda, and nutmeg. You can sift them, but very few people sift any more.

3. Stir the flour blend into the first bowl, and add vanilla.

4. Chill for at least two hours. Overnight works best.

5. Preheat oven to 350°F.

6. Roll into balls the size of walnuts. Line up each ball on cookie sheet.

7. Use a drinking glass to flatten each ball.

8. Bake for 10 to 12 minutes.

Icing

Sometimes you just need to make icing and you ain't got time to be messing around.

1 box (16 ounces) powdered sugar

1/2 cup of frozen strawberries, thawed

3/4 stick of butter, softened

1. In a large bowl, combine sugar, strawberries and butter. Mix until you get the right consistency for spreading.

Caramel Buttermilk Icing

1 stick (1/2 cup) oleo (margarine or butter)
1 cup buttermilk
2 cup powdered sugar
1 teaspoon soda pop
1 teaspoon vanilla extract

1. In a small pan melt oleo.

2. Add buttermilk, sugar and soda pop and heat until combined. Do not let it boil. Stir constantly.

3. Pour into a mixing bowl that can handle hot liquid.

4. Add vanilla. Beat and add sugar to get right consistency for spreading.

Fresh Strawberry Cake

1 box white cake mix
13 ounce box Jello
1 cup vegetable oil
1 cup frozen strawberries, thawed
4 eggs

1. Preheat the oven to 350°F.

2. Flour and grease a cake pan.

3. In a large bowl, combine cake mix and Jello. While stirring with a mixer, add oil, strawberry, and eggs.

4. Pour batter into the cake pan.

5. Bake for 30 minutes.

Single Pie Crust

1 1/3 cup flour, sifted
1/2 teaspoon salt
1/3 cup shortening
3 tablespoon cold water

1. Combine flour and salt in bowl, add shortening and blend well.

2. Add water, make into a ball and roll out as you normally do.

Fresh Strawberry Pie

9-inch pie crust, cooked
3 ounces cream cheese
1 pint strawberries (crushed)
1 pint whole strawberries
1 cup sugar
2 teaspoons cornstarch
2 cups whipped cream

1. Line bottom of cooked pie crust with cream cheese.

2. Arrange whole strawberries on top.

3. In a pan, heat crushed strawberries, sugar, and cornstarch and cook until thickened.

4. Remove from heat and allow to cool for 20 minutes or so.

5. Pour over whole berries, top with whip cream.

6. Cool before serving.

Egg Custard Pie

4 eggs
1/2 cup sugar
1/2 teaspoon salt
3 cups milk, scalded
1 teaspoon vanilla extract
1/4 teaspoon nutmeg
1 pie crust, uncooked

1. Preheat oven to 400°F.

2. In a large bowl, beat eggs slightly.

3. Mix in sugar and salt. Continue mixing and add milk.

4. When all the ingredients are mixed well, pour into pie crust and sprinkle with nutmeg.

5. Bake until pie is set, about 25 - 30 minutes.

Sweet Potato Pie

Growing up, the saying "mom and apple pie" made no sense to me. Sweet potato pie is the American dessert. Maybe pecan pie. But definitely not apple pie.

Here's a recipe that will allow you to do the fourth of July right.

1 1/2 cups sweet potatoes, cooked and mashed
2/3 cups brown sugar
1 teaspoon ground cinnamon
1/4 teaspoon salt
1 egg
1/2 teaspoon nutmeg
1 cup milk
1/3 cup butter
1 pie crust, uncooked

1. Preheat oven to 350°F.

2. In a large bowl, mix sweet potatoes, sugar, cinnamon, salt, egg, nutmeg, milk, and butter.

3. Pour into pie crust.

4. Bake for one hour.

Dessert Salad

1 large can (12 ounces) pineapple chunks, drained
       or 1 1/2 cups of fresh pineapple, chopped
1 carton (8 ounces) whipped cream - I use Cool Whip
1 can cherry pie filling
1 can (14 ounces) condensed milk
1 cup chopped pecans

1. In a large bowl, stir whipped cream, cherry pie filling, milk, and pecans.

2. When mixed together, stir in pineapple.

3. Set in refrigerator overnight and serve cold.

Corn Pudding

2 cans corn (creamed)
1 tablespoon flour
1 tablespoons sugar
2 eggs
salt and pepper to taste
1 tablespoons of Worcestershire sauce
1/2 cup milk
1/4 cup butter

1. Preheat oven to 350°F.

2. In a large bowl, mix corn, flour, sugar, eggs, Worcestershire sauce, milk and butter.

3. Pour into a 9 by 13-inch casserole dish.

4. Bake uncovered for one hour.

Banana Nut Pancakes

1 3/4 cups flour
2 teaspoons sugar
1 1/2 teaspoons baking powder
1 teaspoon baking soda
2 eggs (well beaten)
2 cups butter milk
3 tablespoons butter
2 cups chopped pecans
2 bananas (sliced)
vegetable oil or butter for cooking

1. In a large bowl, combine flour, eggs, baking powder, and baking soda.

2. Beat in eggs and milk to complete the batter.

3. Pour batter into a hot oiled pan to make pancakes like you normally would.

4. Before flipping place banana slices and sprinkle nuts on uncooked side.

5. After flipping pancake, cook about four minutes or until golden brown.

6. Serve hot with your favorite syrup or honey.

Rice Pudding

1 cup rice
3 egg
4 cups milk
1 teaspoon vanilla
1 teaspoon cinnamon
pinch salt
butter for greasing casserole dish

1. Preheat oven to 325°F.

2. Cook rice until tender and done.

3. Using a colander, rinse rice with hot water.

4. Grease a casserole dish with butter and pour in an even layer of rice.

5. In a medium bowl, beat eggs well.

6. Add sugar, salt, and milk.

7. Pour over rice in casserole dish and swirl gently with fork. Sprinkle with cinnamon.

8. Bake in oven for 1 hour.

Pound Cake

1 pound butter

3 cups sugar

6 eggs

4 cups flour

1 teaspoon vanilla

1 cup milk (whole or 2%)

shortening or oil to grease Bundt pan

1. Preheat the oven to 350°F.

2. In a medium-sized bowl, cream butter and sugar until no grain can be felt. To do this, gently mash sugar into butter with a fork and then with a wooden spoon, stir until butter is light and fluffy.

3. Beat in eggs one at a time. Continue beating and slowly add flour one cup at time.

4. Beat in milk until smooth.

5. Pour into a greased Bundt cake pan.

6. Bake for 1 1/2 hours.

7. When cool, serve with vanilla ice cream, because it's vanilla ice cream.

Buttermilk Pound Cake

1 cup shortening

3 cups sugar

6 eggs

1 teaspoon vanilla

3 cups flour

1 cup buttermilk

1/2 teaspoon salt

1/2 teaspoon baking soda

1. Preheat oven to 350°F.

2. Cream shortening and sugar. To do this, gently mash sugar into butter with a fork and then with a wooden spoon, and stir until butter is light and fluffy.

3. While mixing, add eggs one at a time.

4. Then add salt, vanilla, and baking soda.

5. Finally, add flour and mix completely.

6. Pour into a greased Bundt pan.

7. Bake for 1 hour.

Sour Cream Pound Cake

1 cup shortening or
    3 sticks margarine (margarine makes the best cake)
6 eggs
3 cups sugar
¼ teaspoon salt
3 cups flour
1/2 teaspoon baking soda
¼ teaspoon vanilla extract

1. Preheat oven to 325°F..

2. Cream shortening and sugar in a large bowl until fluffy. To do this, gently mash sugar into butter with a fork and then with a wooden spoon, stir until butter is light and fluffy.

3. While mixing, add eggs one at a time.

4. Add flour and sour cream.

5. When batter is mixed well, pour into a greased and floured Bundt pan.

6. Bake for 1 ½ hours.

Strawberry Pound Cake

1 box yellow cake mix

1 package strawberry Jello instant pudding mix

6 eggs

½ cup vegetable oil

¾ cup strawberry nectar

1. Preheat oven to 300°F.

2. In a large bowl, combine cake mix, Jello, oil, and strawberry nectar.

3. While mixing, add eggs one at a time. Continue mixing until batter is light and creamy

4. Pour into a lightly floured cake pan.

5. Bake for 45 minutes.

7-Up Pound Cake

3 cups sugar

3 sticks butter

6 eggs

3 cups flour

1 cup 7-Up (any clear soda pop will work)

1 teaspoon vanilla extract

1 teaspoon lemon juice

1. Preheat oven to 350°F.

2. In a large bowl, cream butter and shortening. To do this, gently mash sugar into butter with a fork and then with a wooden spoon, stir until butter is light and fluffy.

3. Add eggs one at a time. Add flour, 7 Up, vanilla, and lemon juice. In a blender, mix well.

4. Bake in a greased and floured Bundt pan for 1 1/2 hours.

Candied Yams

4 medium-sized sweet potatoes
1/2 cup water
1 cup sugar
dash salt
1 teaspoon vanilla
1 teaspoon cinnamon
6 tablespoons butter

1. Wash, peel and cut potatoes.

2. Put water and sugar in pot and boil potatoes until potatoes are tender.

3. Add salt, vanilla, cinnamon, and butter.

4. Cook for 15 boiling the liquid into a syrup.

Chocolate Popsicles

2 teaspoon flour
2/3 cup sugar
1 tablespoon cocoa powder
dash salt
2 cups milk (whole or 2%)
1 large can (12 ounces) evaporated milk
wooden or plastic popsicle sticks

5. In a sauce pan, mix flour, sugar, cocoa powder, whole milk, and salt.

6. Cook over medium heat until thick. Stir constantly. Do not allow to boil or scorch.

7. Remove from heat, stir in evaporated milk.

8. Pour into molds and place the sticks.

LAST WORDS

✓ The bible like a bank is most helpful when it is open.
✓ If you can't sleep, don't count sheep; talk to the shepherd.

Bible Verses: Emergency numbers to "call"...

✓ when your prayers grow narrow or selfish, call Psalm 67.
✓ when you feel down and out, call Romans 8 vs 31-39.
✓ if your pocket book is empty, call Psalm 37.
✓ if people seem unkind, call John 15.
✓ if you want to be fruitful, call John 15.
✓ when you are lonely and fearful, call Psalm 23.
✓ if you are depressed, call Psalm 27.
✓ for a great invitation, call Isaiah 55.
✓ when your prayer grows narrow or selfish, call Psalm 67.
✓ for Paul's secret to happiness, call Colossians 3: 12-17.

ABOUT THE AUTHOR

Wilma was born in Newport, Arkansas. She attended Branch High, a segregated school, and completed her degree at Arkansas Baptist College in Little Rock, Arkansas. She married Raymond J. Miller soon after graduation.

While working at Timex and Silverwood Industries, she raised three children while perfecting her recipes at home, family reunions, and church event.

Even after the death of her husband to heart disease and daughter to cancer, retirement has not slowed Wilma at all. Late in life; she started a new career as a caregiver and author.

Wilma is also a performance artist specializing in religious comedy.

Momma's Home Cooking is her first book.